Offerings

The Way of the Andean Despacho Ceremony

A Visual Journey
Nourishing + Healing + Connecting + Honoring
Returning to Essence

Barbara Swift

For Ryan
1978-2018

Introduction

I began creating this little book in January of 2021, a year into the pandemic that stopped the whole world in its tracks, and as I was approaching the milestone of turning 70. In all the quiet hours spent in relative isolation, I did a lot of reflection. I asked myself questions, the big questions. What do I want to leave as a legacy? How can I best serve? In what ways can my life experience benefit others? How do I make difference? How can I inspire others? How do I want to be remembered by my children, grandchildren, and beyond? These are the questions that rattle around in my head for hours on end.

There is so much pain, loss, loneliness and uncertainty in these incredible times we're in, and it seems sometimes there is nowhere to go to escape. The entire world is in this thing together. Mother Nature/La Maestra Ultima/Madre Naturaleza/Pachamama... the ultimate teacher has given us hard lessons, a very challenging time-out, and has delivered some devastating consequences for our collective behavior over centuries.

As I sit with all of this, my senses have been awakened as never before, and awareness is growing day by day. Spring of 2020 brought a global pandemic, and with it, much suffering. Yet, during that time, a glorious display of beauty unfolded, in the form of nature expressing herself fully. I marinated in it —quietly allowing, listening, seeing, feeling, praying, sensing, crying, laughing, shedding, clearing, singing, grieving, celebrating.

Our family has had some unimaginable losses in the past few years, yet I am aware that I am very fortunate, as I sit in my backyard on a hill overlooking Los Angeles. I ask myself more questions: How can I be of service to those who are without resources: the homeless, the dying, the ones who have lost loved ones or livelihoods, the fragile, the lonely, the essential workers, the frontline saviors, the vulnerable? These questions sometimes haunt me. All I know for now is to take a cue from Mother Nature and be responsible for myself, to my family and all my beloveds, transforming into the truest and fullest expression of my own potential; to be like a lighthouse, a clear light to illuminate the way forward, to give when and where I can, to share my resources with a spirit of generosity.

We have to bloom. May we all bloom together, out of the mud, like the lotus.

I share here my own experience, which is really all I have, in hopes it may provide beauty, inspiration and comfort. For me, ritual and ceremony have helped me navigate all that has transpired over the last few years. Ceremony is a way of escaping ordinary reality, of transcending the struggle, if only for a little while. In that little while, healing can happen, as we are connecting with a power greater than ourselves, and those connections grow and deepen. There comes a time when we become aware we are not alone, we are being held by unconditional love, by Spirit in many forms.

Ritual and ceremony have provided solace, a sense of connection, and powerful healing for me, and one of the most empowering, soothing and healing practices I know is creating despachos, which are prayer offerings made with flowers, leaves, sweets and other items related to the purpose of the offering. Despachos are a representation of our relations, beautiful little altars representing the cosmos and our own place in creation. They are done for a multitude of reasons and for many occasions: to dialog with Spirit, to heal, to connect with nature, to transform, to celebrate, to honor, to manifest. They are offerings from the heart, soulful expressions of gratitude, and a way of coming into right relationship with Life itself. With each offering, each ceremony, I was able to walk through the past six years of profound loss in our family, beginning with my sister's husband's death in 2015, followed by the death of my mother in 2016, the untimely deaths in my daughter-in-law's family, and then, the most profound loss of all for me and my husband, the sudden death of our son in 2018.

After a year of processing that devastating loss, the pandemic hit.

When the noise and chaos of the world feels unsettling, confusing, relentless and

unbearable, when all that we thought we knew seems an illusion, there is a place to go. That place is within, it is the place where the soul resides, the vast and open space of potential, of possibility, of depth and meaning.

As I look through all the photos on my phone's camera roll, I see hundreds of pictures of despacho ceremonies over the years, which, one ceremony at a time, helped me feel grounded and tethered in the belly of the land/Pachamama. I have been held and protected by Mother Nature and Spirit. The anger, grief, despair, fear and devastation after my son's death slowly transformed into renewed energy and an even stronger sense of being connected with something much greater than my little self. As I fed the land with my prayers, my sorrow, and tears, I was nourished and consoled and made whole again by Mother Earth and Spirit.

What gets me through these incredibly

difficult times is deepening my relationship with Spirit/Mother Nature/Pachamama, as well as taking care of relationships with beloveds on a daily basis. I've also been listening intently and learning from those whose lineage has been profoundly impacted by multi-generational disenfranchisement and trauma. I've learned so much from them, and I aspire to be more generous with my personal resources and energy.

Being awake, aware and available to others, and to Spirit; being willing to release all that no longer serves either myself or the greater collective; being open to change; and having the courage to live with complete honesty and authenticity...all of these create the foundation of a new way of being on the other side of the great dismemberment of life as we've known it.

In each and every despacho, I offer so much love and gratitude to my mentors: the Peruvian/Andean medicine people, and the Winged Ones: the Apus/mountain spirits and Santa Tierras/feminine earth spirits.

These past years have brought, along with immense pain, fear, suffering and loss, the realization that our old ways of being and relating, through rugged individualism and separation, do not serve.

Love, wisdom, compassion, and generosity of spirit will provide the threads from which the new consciousness will be woven.

It is my hope that this little book will inspire, teach, console and make available practical and beautiful ways of navigating the challenges life brings, especially now. I hope you may find in these pages a practice that works for you, a practice that will lead you back to your own essence, to your heart, to your innocence. May you feel comforted, may you feel the embrace of Spirit, may you find connection to loved ones who have passed, may you find joy and beauty, may you be empowered, may you call your soul back home.

Beginnings

In 2011, in Joshua Tree, California, I sat at a little table across from an Andean paqo, the Quechua word for shaman, while he prepared for me a traditional despacho, the purpose of which was to bring me into right relationship with Mother Earth and all my relations; and to bring success, abundance and good fortune in the areas of home, family, health and money.

The shaman was dressed in the traditional clothing of the high Peruvian Andes: shorts, sandals, a brightly colored hand-woven poncho and the most colorful hat with long tassels on the ear flaps, and pompoms of yarn on the top. He placed a square of white paper on a beautiful hand woven textile. He poured sugar in the shape of a cross in the center, which represents the Southern Cross, and in the four quadrants created by the cross, he placed rice, seeds, grains, and incense in a mandala-like pattern, with a shell in the middle.

He spoke only Quechua, so he handed me 5 sets of coca leaves in groups of three leaves, pointed to a little paper with the words Family, Health, Home, Money, Spirit written on it, and conveyed to me use my breath to blow my prayers for each of the categories into each of the fanned out 3-leaf sets, which I later learned are called 'kintus'. He blew his own prayers into additional kintus, placed them in a circle around the little shell, along with mine, then placed red and white carnations all around. It looked so beautiful!
Next, he began to add more, and more, and more, and let me tell you, there were some really odd things like llama fat and a dried up thing I later learned was a piece of an unborn llama fetus.

I was fascinated, and at the same time, wondering how on earth I ended up here in this crazy ceremony. More things piled on, like candies in the shape of cars and houses and people, little metal objects representing all kinds of things, animal cookies, sweet wafers, crackers, confetti, neon-colored candies, more sugar, red and white ribbons, fake $100 dollar bills, mica, raisins, dried figs, and various other oddities that I couldn't name. Lastly, he placed a rainbow of yarn arched above the top, and covered the whole thing with cotton, and a big starfish on top. He rang a little brass bell over it, then wrapped it all up like a present, tied it up with twine, and handed it to me.

I would burn it later that evening at our fire ceremony. The fire would devour the sacred bundle and with the smoke, dispatch all the prayers to the spirits, who would help them manifest. At that moment in time, I had no inkling as to how I would come to embrace this simple and beautiful practice, how meaningful it would become, and how creating despachos in a deeply ceremonial way would help me, my family and those I would come to serve, to heal and connect with Nature. It became a regular practice that grew more powerful through the years, and brought me solace and personal healing in ways I never would have imagined.

The Despacho Ceremony

Preparation: Creating Sacred Space

Gather up all the ingredients you'll be using and place them around a beautiful ceremonial cloth on the floor or table, or outside on the ground. Light a candle. You may want to burn a little sage around the room or outdoor space, and perhaps smudge yourself and all participants before beginning the ceremony.

Invite Spirit into your space. Invite God/Great Spirit/Creator/Buddha/Christ, by whatever name resonates with you. Invite all spirit helpers. You may want to use a bell or rattle while you call in spirits by name. Be clear in your intention for the ceremony, and ask for assistance from the spirit world. Be true to your own belief system, your own faith.

Here is an example, the way I open space: I place my hand on Mother Earth, ring a little bell or rattle, and spritz Agua de Florida on the ground or floor. I say something like this: "Santa Tierra Pachamama, Santa Tierra Madre, sweet unconditional Mother, Mother that has never left us, Mother that will never leave us, we call on your Presence. Be with us. Embrace us as we prepare this offering, wrap us in your love, wrap us in your healing, wrap us in your wisdom. Mamacocha, great mother of all the waters, we call on your presence. Wash us clean, with your great waves of compassion." Then I call on feminine spirits of the land that are personal to me, my local Santa Tierra that inhabits the land on which we live, with whom I have a relationship. And I call on the Divine Mother in all her forms: Guadalupe, Lourdes, Fatima, Kwan Yin, and others.

Next, I rattle or ring a bell and spritz toward the sky, calling on Great Spirit in all forms:

"Great Spirit, Creator, Mother/Father God, Great Mystery, You who are known by a thousand names, we call on your Presence. Bring your light, your blessing, be with us here. Bring us your healing energies, your care and protection." I then call in the Apus/Mountain Spirits with whom I have a personal relationship, and ask to be wrapped in their wings of light.

Despacho Ingredients

Everything that goes into a despacho has meaning. Each item is symbolic, a representation of an aspect of life, a relationship, a prayer, a vision. In the creation of the layers of our offering, we build a representation of the cosmos: the lower, middle and upper worlds. We also address the past and our ancestral lineages, the present time and our relationships, our health; and we create and call in a vision for the time to come.

Each item that goes into the offering is infused with intention and meaning through the breath, blowing into each item before it is placed. The overall purpose of our offering is to come into right relationship with everything, strengthen our relationship with Spirit, and bring abundance and well-being through love and gratitude. Following is a list of items that go into a traditional despacho offering with a short description of their symbolic meanings.

Large white paper
The blank canvas on which the despacho will be created, and which will wrap around the offering and be tied with ribbon or string.

Sugar
The foundation for life, love, sweetness. Can also represent the snows, glaciers.

Rice
Sustenance, nutrition, energy, abundance, fertility, the reproductive principle.

Amaranth / Quinoa
The high protein, extremely nutritious grains that represent the highest, purest, most refined light, sustenance.

Corn
Life-giving, nutritious energy, symbolic of right action, work, fruits of our labors.

Shell
The mother of all the waters. The matrix of creation, the cosmic womb of the Great Mother. Usually, candy dolls are placed into the shell, representing the feminine and masculine principles, woman and man, coming together to create new life. I use little Guatemalan "worry dolls" when I can't find candy dolls.

Llama fat
The energy that animates all aspects of life. This can also be replaced by wild animal fat or jerky.

Llama fetus
The incubation of us and our visions in the belly of Mother Earth/Pachamama, representing the unborn. This is used in Peru, but pretty impossible to find else-where. Jerky can be used as a replacement.

Sage
Sacred, cleansing aromatic herb that calls Spirit.

Incense and aromatic herbs
These make a wonderful smell when burned, and, mixed with the sugar, the fragrance entices and invites the spirits of Pachamama and the Apus/mountain spirits to come to feast on our offering.

Coca leaves or bay leaves
In groups of three, they become "kintus", which receive and contain our prayers, through our breath.

Beans and seeds
Seeds of love, seeds of fruition, seeds of new visions, sacred connections to our lineages.

Coca seeds or tobacco
The sacred, reciprocity for what has been given to us by Spirit.

Flowers
Red and white flowers are gifts of love to the feminine and masculine principles. Flowers of all kinds and colors are used to remember and call in our healed and fulfilled states, and are the calling in of beauty.

Dried figs and raisins
Our ancestors, and the ancestral lineages of the land, who are called to assist us, and to whom we give our love, thanks and gratitude.

Alphabet noodles
Communication, right language, the language of the heart.

Animal crackers
The animal kingdom, the wild and the domesticated.

Large round cracker
Collectivity, oneness, the community, the village, the Whole.

Candies
Love, sweetness, all our relations in harmony.

Candy or chocolate frogs
The cycles of water, transformation, keepers of the rain.

Silver and gold rods
The sounds of the land, dialoguing with the animated universe.

Mica
Lost soul parts, the calling back of lost energetic pieces of ourselves, protecting and strengthening our energy body/anima/soul.

Lodestone or magnetite
Attracting that which is wanted and needed, repelling that which is unwanted or harmful.

Gold and silver beads
The sun and the moon.

Gold and silver paper
The masculine energies of knowledge and the mystical, the feminine energies of the magical.

Gold and silver threads
Sacred, energetic, luminous lines of connection.

Little candles
Light, fire, the solar plexus, vitality.

Wayrurus
Red seeds with black dots, from the Amazon jungle, bringing good fortune, balance and equilibrium.

White cotton
The clouds, cycles of water through rain, the heavens, the upper domains of the spirit, luminous awareness.

Rainbow yarn
The rainbow bridge, the bridge that connects all worlds, the lower, middle and upper realms.

Confetti paper
Celebration, joy, homecoming, honoring our journey and all our relations.

Starfish
The remembering of our origin, and where we will return—to the stars. Remembering our place in creation.

Red and white wine
To sprinkle on the completed despacho, to honor and bless the earth and the heavens.

Creating the Despacho

The following general guidelines are for an offering that is done for connection and creating right relationship, called an Ayni despacho. "Ayni" is a Quechua word meaning reciprocity, balance, harmony, sacred exchange. It is done often, and is a way of honoring and giving gratitude for our lives, for all the gifts, blessings, healing and nourishment from Mother Nature/Pachamaama/Spirit. My own despacho offerings are grounded in the traditional Andean ceremonies, yet there are some differences, in keeping with what is natural and indigenous to North America.

Place a square of white paper, the size depending on how big the despacho will be, onto your ceremonial cloth. For water despachos or offerings that will be buried, I use giant bird of paradise or banana leaves, big enough to wrap around the completed despacho. A big round loaf of bread can also be used for water despachos, as is done in the Andes.

Begin with a base of sugar, representing sweetness, love. I place the sugar in the shape of a cross, that represents the Southern Cross constellation. This creates four quadrants, representing the four-chambered universe, the four-chambered heart.

Place rice, grains, beans, corn in the quadrants. Use the breath to blow your intention and blessing into each ingredient before it is placed. Place a shell, representing the ocean, the womb of the Mother, in the middle.

Use candy dolls or representations of the masculine and feminine principles inside the shell.

Sprinkle fragrant herbs such as lavender, sage and sacred tobacco all around. Use herbs and fragrances indigenous to the local natural environment.

Use bay leaves in groups of three, called kintus, with stems down and leaves face up in a fanned out manner, and use your breath to blow heartfelt prayers into the kintus. Kintus can also be made from rose petals, also in groups of three petals. Place them in the despacho all around the shell. These will be your prayers with the purpose of the despacho in mind; for honoring, for healing, for connecting, for expressing gratitude, for celebration. Prayers will be both personal and on behalf of the collective.

Add flowers, herbs, candies, sparkly things, gold and silver threads, animal cookies, butterflies, stars, little candles, gummy frogs, mica, glitter, magnetite, confetti, whatever meaningful representations you have, of things you want to address. Remember to use your breath to inform and set intention for each of the items that go into your offering. Let it be an expression of your strong intent, let it be an act of beauty, love and creativity.

Wrap rainbow colored yarn around the perimeter, representing the rainbow bridge that connects all worlds. Cover the whole creation with cotton, representing the clouds, and place a starfish in the center, representing the heavens, and the stars from which we come.

Sprinkle red wine on the despacho, first blessing the wine with your breath, and asking for blessings from Spirit. Wrap the paper around the despacho and tie it with twine or yarn. The despacho is then placed into a ceremonial fire, which consumes the offering, transmutes and disperses the prayers, transforming the physical into light and energy. Some despachos are released into water, some are buried in the earth.

Despachos for Grief, Loss, and Remembrance

"There is a sacredness in tears. They are not the mark of weakness, but of power. They are messengers of overwhelming grief and of unspeakable love."

~ Washington Irving

In the early hours of the morning, on August 14, 2018, we got a phone call that changed our family's life forever. Our son, Ryan, had died in the night, leaving behind his beautiful wife; his sweet, innocent, smart-as-a-whip 3 year-old son; a baby girl on the way; shattered parents; devastated brothers; all of his family, friends, hospital work colleagues, and patients who loved him. Having one of my children die was always something I believed I couldn't survive. Yet here I am, here we are, healing, learning, moving forward, having been held with fierce love from our ayllu, which, in Quechua, means tribe/community/a collective.

I've known all about the classic stages of grief, and learned about the process in theory. I've sat at the bedside as my parents, brothers-in-law, and close friends took their last breath. Nothing prepared me for this one, though.

Grief is not linear. It's complicated. It's individual and personal. I was shattered, devastated, broken, dismembered by Ryan's death. Yet I can say I am whole again, by no means the same, but healed, transformed, re-membered. Today, I am profoundly sad, I miss Ryan terribly;

and I am grateful, filled with awe and wonder, empowered and fueled by all the love that has put us back together again.

Our new little granddaughter came 16 days early, on the very last minute of her daddy's birthday. Whoa.

Spirit embraces us and speaks in powerful ways.

After Ryan's death, my close friends circled around me and our family and simply asked what I/we needed. The first thing I asked was for them to do a grief ceremony on the beach with my husband and me.

We created a despacho, with so much love, so many prayers for Ryan, to honor his life and to ask that his soul find its way across the rainbow bridge to meet his ancestors on the other side. We asked for solace, compassion and deep healing for our entire family: brothers, sisters-in-law, nieces, nephews, aunts, uncles, and for Ryan's wife, son, and unborn daughter.

Our offering, to be given to Mother Ocean, was made out of prayers and tears. We filled it with flowers, kintus of bay leaves, sugar and candies. Each kintu and item was infused with our intent and breath. When complete, we wrapped it all up in giant bird of paradise leaves. Bob, my husband, waded out into the water, and released it beyond the waves.

Then we had a feast, there on the beach, as the sun was setting and the sky turned gold. There were sunbeams coming down onto the water, spirits in the form of birds flying overhead, and a full moon rose. There were no words to express the depth of feeling and the love in that sweet, powerful ceremony. It was a timeless moment of deep connection for which the mind has limited capacity to embrace.

Only the heart and soul can meet and process such a profound experience.
That ceremony, 10 days after Ryan's passing, was the beginning of my healing.

There is much to grieve, and much to be born out of our collective grief. May all our tears be sacred tears, may they flow freely, may they cleanse the earth, and ease the pain that comes with death and loss; and the pain that comes with birth, the birthing of a compassionate new world.

May you find peace.
May you find healing.
May you find wisdom.
May you find love.

Ceremony of Remembrance

Healing Despachos

Despachos are one of the healing approaches used by Andean healers and medicine people. These healing bundles address all forms of dis-ease, whether it be in the realm of the physical, emotional, soul or spirit. There may be physical illness, depression, apathy, loss of purpose, lack of fulfillment, soul loss, a myriad of other maladies.

Healing despachos are also used for the dying, and after a person has died, to clear the heavy energies that may be interfering with the dying process, or to assist the soul in making the transition and journey to the other side. In Andean cosmology, this passage is seen as crossing the rainbow bridge, to the land of the ancestors that reside in the upper world, the Hanaqpacha.

A white healing despacho for a friend.

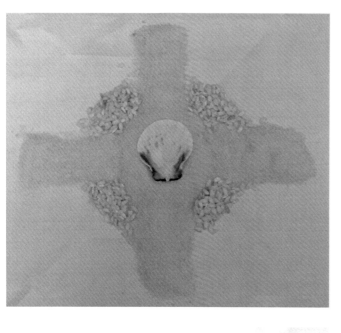 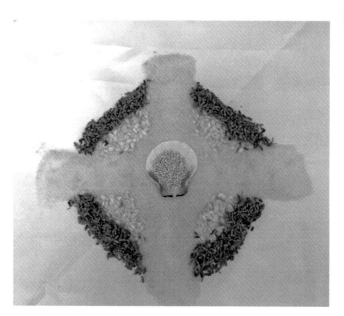

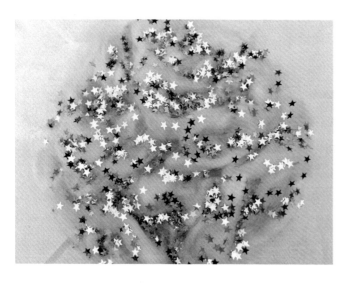 

This is a healing despacho created for my 94 year-old mother as she was dying, filled with prayers for her fulfillment and a peaceful journey across the Rainbow Bridge.

The cotton gets rubbed all over the body, and up and down the spine, to absorb heavy energy.

The kintus are bay leaves and rose petals.

Vesica Piscis Despacho

During the pandemic, I joined with a group of my fellow travelers to do special ceremonies creating despachos using sacred geometry. The intention of these ceremonies was to envision the structure and architecture of a new way of being for the world.

We focused on:

The time past and the time to come, where we've been and where we're going...a new map.

Re-visioning our world.

Co-creating with Spirit.

The lens through which new vision comes.

The birth canal, the opening/portal to new consciousness.

Gratitude for learning from direct experience and divine direction.

Clarity of vision.

Creation of new cekes/energetic lines of connection.

Prayers for the new world emerging.

Prayers of release.

Holding space for healing fully and completely.

Honoring the Feminine

Blossoming and blooming into fulfillment.

Layer by layer, we heal, release and rebirth consciousness.

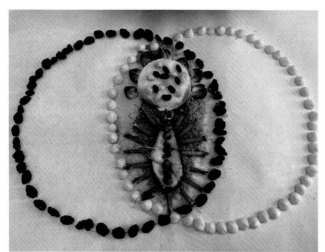

Honoring the Elements

May I embody the Land ~ nourishing

Mother Earth bringing new life, healing, strength,
compassion, and groundedness.

May I embody the Waters ~ flowing

Moving freely through life, bringing softness,
strength; shaped, not held, by whatever is containing
me as I pass through.

May I embody Air ~ cleansing

the great winds clearing what has become
stagnant, breathing new life, bringing clarity,
new visions into being.

May I embody Fire ~ warming

Illuminating, purifying, transmuting, transforming
through my being and my actions.

May I embody Grandmother Moon ~ reflecting

Reflecting the fire and pure light of the sun,
a mirror, and perfect reflection of all that is.

**With gentleness and clarity
may I light the way.**

Honoring Water

Ceremonial offering to call for rain and snow in California,
for the return of the natural cycles of water all around the world.

Here, a despacho is created calling on the memory of water in a dry creek bed.

Offerings to honor water typically contain white and/or yellow flowers and are full of sweets. I like to wrap them in large leaves before placing them into Mother Ocean.

In the Andes, water despachos are created on round loaves of bread and placed into streams, lakes, and rivers.

Honoring Fire

During the devastating fires all over the Southwestern United States and in Peru, we created despacho offerings that held prayers honoring the elements of Fire and Air. We also included prayers for our own personal transformation, asking for any outrage and fear to be transmuted into passion, compassion, love, and Right Action.

Despachos to Fire contain fresh fruits in addition to other traditional ingredients and are always burned in a ceremonial fire, preferably on a Full Moon.

A Year of Ceremony

January

February

March

Spring Equinox

April

May

June

Summer Solstice

July

August

September

Autumn Equinox

October

November

December

Winter Solstice

Ceremony with Children

> "Where ritual is absent, the young ones are restless or violent, there are no real elders, and the grown-ups are bewildered. The future is dim."
>
> ~ **Malidoma Patrice Some, Ritual~Power, Healing, and Community**

Kids are so open to ceremony and celebrating Nature. My grandchildren love to make despachos.

A few years ago, we made one in the backyard, and as soon as we were finished my granddaughter said, "can we make another one?"

With kids, I keep the process very simple, with flowers, leaves, sugar, rice, candies, chocolate, seeds, sage, and lavender, and topped with cotton clouds and glittery stars and confetti. We make them during the day, then look forward to making a ceremonial fire after dinner, which includes rattles and songs. One particular night, our 4 year-old grandson led us in the song, "Baby Beluga" and then we placed our offering in the fire.

"Wisdom is encoded in beauty."
~ The Andean Masters

Post Script

It is now April, 2023.

The past winter brought incredible, historic rains and snow here in California, that quenched the thirst of the land. The hills are alive, vibrantly green, with flowers blooming everywhere. New life has emerged, and it seems miraculous to me. Mother Nature is fully expressing her wild and magnificent beauty, the beauty beyond imagination. She is answering our collective prayers.

My hope and prayer is that we all become the fullest and truest expressions all that we are, and all we were meant to be. May we share with the world our own unique gifts and talents. May we come together in love and gratitude, to plant new seeds for our future, toward our collective well-being and fulfillment.

May we grow, may we shine, may we blossom, may we bloom.

Thank You

To my family: my husband, Bob; my sons, Ryan, Timothy, and Jonathan; my daughters-in-law, Jessica, Monique, and Yali; my grandchildren, Sophia, Alexa, Jon Ryan, Sean, Coen, and Georgia.

To my ayllu, all of whom I love deeply, you are my soul brothers and sisters.

To my Peruvian medicine teachers, your generosity, love, wisdom and teachings have changed my life.

To Jose Luis Herrera, you brought the magical and mystical into my and my family's lives...and profound healing. There are no words big enough to express my love and gratitude.

To Tatjana Jakob Herrera, you are a beloved sister, healer, teacher, friend and have brought incredible beauty, healing, laughter and wisdom into my life.

To Jessica Swift, my gratitude is immense for all the work you did in designing and putting this book together for me... and the healing that has happened in the process is immeasurable.

This book is my offering.

With immense love and gratitude,

Barbara